Dorothy does a great job, with this being her first book, opening the doors for her heart demonstrating how God can turn a life thought to be doomed, into a life of victory that is being used for ministry to help others. This is a required reading for anyone, male or female, who has experienced separation or divorce, and you're left feeling empty, alone, or betrayed. Dorothy has researched scriptural foundations relevant to her personal experiences, and she shares how God can do a "new thing" in terms of relationships, particularly with Him, in those who are willing.

Daphene O. Singleton, Ph.D., D.Min
Educator, Bible Teacher, & Motivational Speaker

LESSONS I
LEARNED
— *in the* —
DARK

DOROTHY PINO

WESTBOW
PRESS®
A DIVISION OF THOMAS NELSON
& ZONDERVAN

WestBow Press books may be ordered through booksellers or by contacting:

WestBow Press
A Division of Thomas Nelson & Zondervan
1663 Liberty Drive
Bloomington, IN 47403
www.westbowpress.com
844-714-3454

ISBN: 978-1-6642-1178-0 (sc)
ISBN: 978-1-6642-1177-3 (hc)
ISBN: 978-1-6642-1179-7 (e)

Library of Congress Control Number: 2020922104

Print information available on the last page.

WestBow Press rev. date: 12/10/2020

I dedicate this book to my friend Adrianne, who saw something in me that I did not see in myself and continued to speak to it until it came to fruition. Thank you. I will be forever grateful.

CONTENTS

Acknowledgments

I want to thank my son, James, and his wife, Amanda, for making a place for me in their home in Montana where I could write this book. It was the perfect place for me to complete this assignment, and I am grateful.

PREFACE

The Lord dropped the idea of writing this book into my spirit several years ago. At the time, I thought it was an idea of mine and did not realize it was of the Lord, so I simply ignored it. Over the years, from time to time, various friends would mention something to me about how I needed to write my book. I still was not convinced God was asking me to do this, so I would tuck the thought away in the back of my mind, not giving it any serious consideration.

I hadn't done much writing over my lifetime and had never thought of myself as a serious author. For this reason, I did not give much attention to the notion of writing a book. When I was in school, I had written some small articles for homework assignments and received encouraging feedback from my instructors, but that was where it ended.

At one point, the Lord downloaded into my spirit the title of the book, *Lessons I Learned in the Dark.* On another occasion, He gave me the title to each chapter, along with scripture references to put just under the chapter titles. I was still not convinced this was something I needed to undertake.

Finally, in the fall of 2019, as I was attending a Wednesday evening church service with a friend in Haltom

City, Texas, she turned to me and said, "The Lord says it's time for you to write that book." That statement got my attention, and on the way home that night, I began to speak to the Lord about the matter. I told Him that I didn't desire to be disobedient, and I knew that if He was truly asking me to write it, then it was because He had need of it. As I do so many times when I sense the Lord asking me to embark on something new or different, I asked Him to give me confirmation from His Word. That Friday morning, as I was in my quiet time, I was reading in Lamentations 3. When I read verse 2, I began to cry as the Holy Spirit caused that verse to jump out at me.

> He has brought me into deepest darkness,
> shutting out all light. (Lamentations 3:2 TLB)

He was giving me the confirmation I had asked for. This verse confirmed the title He had given me for the book, but He didn't stop there. I continued to read, and as I read verses 21–23, I was again stirred in my spirit because He had told me that one of the chapters of the book was to be on His faithfulness. Verse 23 TLB reads, "Great is his faithfulness; his loving-kindness begins afresh each day."

This was confirmation for the title of chapter 2. The final confirmation He gave me that morning concerned what He had instructed me to put on the back cover regarding prayer. That reads, "Have you ever been in a place in your life where darkness was all around you, and the heavens felt like brass over you? Did your prayers seem to hit that brass canopy and fall right back down?"

To confirm this section of the book, He spoke to me through Lamentations 3:44 TLB, which reads, "You have veiled yourself as with a cloud so that our prayers do not reach through."

By the time I had read this third and final confirmation, I was weeping before the Lord and repenting for not giving this assignment serious attention sooner. It was so kind of Him to consider my insecurities concerning writing and show His kindness to me by giving me the confirmations I needed. He had been gently wooing me for approximately five years. Now He was speaking loud and clear, and I knew it. I simply responded, "Yes, Lord!"

I immediately began to rearrange things in my life so I could set time apart for the writing of this book. I must say I have thoroughly enjoyed the experience, and I know now that this is only the beginning.

INTRODUCTION

If you are holding this book in your hands, then I believe that God has a breakthrough in store for you as you read it. Somewhere within these pages lies an answer, an encouragement, hope restored, or strength renewed. My prayer for the reader is that whatever situation you may be facing, you will find the courage to walk it through to victory as you read my story of God's faithfulness to me. He'll do the same for you.

1

CAUGHT OFF GUARD

For man does not know his time. Like fish which are taken in an evil net, and like birds which are caught in a snare, so the sons of man are snared at an evil time, when it suddenly falls upon them.
—ECCLESIASTES 9:12 (RSV)

At the age of twenty, I married my high school sweetheart. James was an upper classman, two years older than me. He was charming, handsome, and strong. He was an athlete, and I loved everything about him—at least everything my eyes could see.

James and I had three children. Our oldest was a daughter, Perri Lynn, and then two sons, James and Jason. I loved our little family and was so happy!

Like all marriages, ours had flaws, and maybe I was a little naive. I always thought that we would work through our problems in time. When we were in our mid-thirties, we both rededicated our lives to the Lord, and our relationship became amazing. It was just what I had been dreaming of since the day we had gotten married twelve years prior. It was like we were on our second honeymoon, but it was better than anything we had ever known before.

We both became very interested in short-term mission trips. Encouraged by our pastor at that time, we went on our first mission trip in October 1996 with a group from our church. The trip was for one week in Thailand and then a second week in Nepal. It was a very different experience for us and unlike anything we had ever done before.

In Thailand, our team ministered to the residents at a home for young girls whose families would have otherwise sold them into sex trafficking. The couple who ran the home would go into the villages and ask the parents of preteen girls if they could take their daughters to live with them, and the couple would teach them a trade. The girls were then taught skills that could be used to get them good paying jobs in the city, such as seamstresses, office clerks, and housekeepers.

The parents were often very agreeable to allowing their daughters to be taught a trade, because the life expectancy of a young girl in the sex trade was very short. Many contracted AIDS or other sexually transmitted diseases that would cut short their lives and their careers. By learning a trade they could use in the business world, the girls were able to earn a good living for many more years, thus helping their families with finances for a longer period of time. James and I both enjoyed our time ministering to those young ladies.

From Thailand we flew to Nepal. After spending a couple of days in Kathmandu to rest, we took a bus out into the countryside of Nepal and then hiked with backpacks through the rice paddies till we made our way into a remote village in the foothills of the Himalaya mountains. Our team of Sherpas had arrived a few hours ahead of us and had set up camp, prepared our dinner, and had it waiting for us when we arrived. It was such a welcomed sight. Everyone on the team was exhausted from the day's events that had brought us there.

On this leg of our mission trip, we were conducting a medical clinic for the village people who lived in that region. The word had spread that medical missionaries were coming from America, and a free clinic would be available to all. As we opened the clinic the next morning, it was overwhelming to see the village people walking to the clinic. There were so many coming from as far as the eye could see. Many had walked for days, carrying their sick and maimed in their arms.

Nepal is a Hindu nation, and they worship many gods or demon spirits. I could feel the darkness and oppression in the atmosphere as we entered their airspace when we were flying into the country. Images of some of the more honored demon spirits were painted on their buildings and on the walls inside their airport. They believed that these spirits would protect them throughout their lives and keep them from harm.

As the people stood in line waiting to be seen by the doctors, we had members of our team who were assigned to lay hands on them and pray over them. Neither James nor I had any medical training, so we were given the assignment to pray over the people. It was during this time that I saw the mighty anointing that was on my husband. When he laid hands on the locals and begin to pray in the name of Jesus, demons would begin to manifest in them. The first time this happened, I heard James cry out, "Oh, Jesus, help me! I don't even know what I am doing!" And of course, Jesus did help.

At that very moment, the lady he was praying for fell to the ground and began to roll around. With great authority, James knelt down beside her and began to command the demons to leave the woman and not come back to her or the daughter who had accompanied the woman to the clinic. As we all watched, the woman instantly became still. She opened her eyes and looked up at us. We were amazed at the transformation in her countenance. The demon spirits had left her as they were commanded to do.

Wow, what a powerful display of deliverance! James and I were amazed at how God had chosen and anointed him for this type of ministry. This experience took us both by surprise, but it also took us to another level of intimacy with God. This was the first of several mission trips James and I would take over the coming years, although this was the only one that we took together.

This new relationship with God and with each other lasted for seven years. Then one day, I noticed James had started drinking again. He was stopping by his favorite bar and shooting pool with his friends, sometimes for hours. He was still attending church with the children and me, but I knew something was desperately wrong. He was slipping back into old behavior patterns from which he had once turned away. At first, I thought it was just a phase. I hoped he would find no satisfaction in those things any longer and would return to the Lord with even greater fervor than before. But the opposite happened. At that time, he accepted a bid on his job with Yellow Freight that would take him away from home on Sundays, making it impossible for us to attend church as a family. Fortunately, the bid lasted only a year. At the end of that year, he bid a position with Sundays off, and once again we were able to attend church together. However, I could tell that our marriage was in trouble. Our relationship was under attack.

In 2004, James took an early retirement from his position at Yellow Freight for medical reasons, but I was still working. Every day while I was at work, I would be tormented with wondering whether my marriage was going to survive this latest onslaught of the enemy. I asked James to go to counseling with me, but he refused, so I went alone.

What I dealt with may not be the same issues you are dealing with. The truth is all of us go through something, and it's different for each of us. We have an enemy, and his name is Satan. He hates us and wants nothing more than to crush us until we are totally destroyed. His goal is to keep us from fulfilling our God-given destinies.

At first, James and I tried to work things out. But he was unwilling to give me the support I needed to restore my hope that we could save our marriage. I was crushed!

Over the next few months, our relationship continued to worsen. I was not willing to continue to live with someone who had become so distant, and I left James. I moved out of the home we were renting at that time and filed for divorce. I had thought that maybe this drastic act on my part would encourage James to seek help or do something that would restore our marriage, but he remained undaunted. In September 2007, our divorce was final.

Our children were already grown and married, and they had children of their own. Both of my sons had received promotions at their jobs, which included transfers to other states. My life that had once seemed so full and rich was suddenly very empty and lonely.

I was fifty-seven years old and starting over—a situation I had never dreamed I would be in. I hadn't planned on this, I hadn't wanted it, and I was devastated. I felt like the air had been knocked out of me, and I couldn't breathe. My cry to the Lord everyday was, "Oh, God, where are You in all this?"

The life I once had no longer existed. My whole world was crumbling around me, and I was not sure I would survive. James was the only man I had ever truly loved, and I couldn't imagine life without him. I chose to trust God to bring me through this dark place, even though He seemed so far away and silent. Charles Spurgeon once said, "To trust God in the light is nothing, but trust Him in the dark—that is faith."[1]

I think what bothered me most about the breakup of our marriage was the fact that I had seen the anointing that was on my husband. I knew this whole thing was a scheme of the enemy to take him out. In other words, the devil was afraid of that anointing. He knew James could and would do damage to his dirty little kingdom if left unchecked. I tried to explain these things to James. I wanted so desperately for him to see what the devil was up to and not give place to his schemes, but he was blinded to the truth. Our whole family was injured because of it.

---

[1] Charles Spurgeon quote from "Quotes About Trusting God," accessed at https://www.biblereasons.com.

DOROTHY PINO

2

GOD IS FAITHFUL

*Yet this I call to mind and therefore I have hope;
because of the Lord's great love, we are not
consumed, for His compassions never fail, they are
new every morning; great is your faithfulness.*
—LAMENTATIONS 3:21–23 (NIV)

Though my life had taken an unexpected turn, I never stopped believing that somehow, someway, God was going to "fix" it. I always believed that James would return to the Lord with the passion he once had, and our marriage would be restored. I simply couldn't believe that it would be any other way. After all, I had seen God answer my prayers over the years and do some amazing things in our family. I had prayed for my husband's salvation for twelve years, and I saw it come to pass. Both of our sons walked away from the Lord in their later teenage years and got into some very harmful lifestyles. I prayed for five years for them to be delivered from the chains of bondage the enemy had gotten them into, and we saw the victory. Praise God! They both returned to the Lord and were radically changed and set free to live very successful lives. God has blessed each of them with a wonderful wife, beautiful children, and a great job to support those families. I am forever grateful for His goodness and mercy to us.

I made many mistakes as a wife and as a mother, but God still answered my prayers. He did so not because of me, but because He is faithful. Even when I am unfaithful, He remains faithful because that's just who He is, and He can't deny Himself (2 Timothy 2:13).

Given my experience of persevering in prayer until I received breakthrough, I was expecting no less on this current situation in my marriage. However, I didn't receive the answer I had hoped for. James dropped completely out of church at that time and began to return to his old lifestyle.

He worked diligently at maintaining a good relationship with our three children and eleven grandchildren. They had become the most important people in his life, and seemingly I had become as nothing.

I have thought of it often since those days: how a woman can give so much of herself for the good of her children and her husband and then be tossed aside like yesterday's newspaper. It's just not right, yet I have since learned that it is more common than one might think. My path has crossed the paths of countless others whose stories are like mine.

James and I had become very distant, seeing each other at weddings and family gatherings. We would always be pleasant but disconnected. We had agreed to be civil to one another for the sake of the children. We wanted to protect them as much as possible from being hurt or injured by our divorce.

Though this was a very emotionally traumatic time in my life, God showed Himself faithful to me on so many levels. I would find verses in the Bible that spoke of His promises to His children, and I would begin to memorize them and quote them daily. One of my favorites is the following.

> I know what I'm doing. I have it all planned out—plans to take care of you, not abandon you, plans to give you the future you hope for. (Jeremiah 29:11 MSG)

DOROTHY PINO

This verse was so special to me because I felt like I had been abandoned by God and everyone else. I felt all alone, and I didn't know how I was going to pull it all together. This verse showed me that I didn't have to try to figure it out. He already had a plan in place, and He would take care of me.

I believe the Bible with all my heart, and I believe that every verse in it is as pertinent for us today as it was for the people it was originally written for so many years ago. In fact, the Bible is one of the main ways that God speaks to us today. Therefore, as I read my Bible daily, I would ask God to speak to me concerning this new season of my life. I would ask Him to show me how I could serve others.

Because I no longer had children at home or a husband to wait on, I began to look for other causes into which I could pour myself. Serving only yourself is a very empty life indeed. I knew He would direct me because He promises to do so in His Word.

One Monday morning as I was driving to work, the emptiness I felt inside became overwhelming. I began to cry bitterly. I pulled my car over to the side of the road in order to gain composure. I yelled out to the Lord and asked Him to please show me what to do with my life. I could not continue to live in such an empty, unfulfilled manner. I sensed in my heart the prompting of the Holy Spirit to call a pastor friend of mine. Upon sharing my heart with this man who knew my situation completely, he suggested that I contact a particular mission's organization in Hawaii and apply to their school. I did so later that day, and within two hours I had a response from them asking me to register for their school.

I knew in my heart this was God's will for me. I completed their online application to attend the Crossroads Discipleship Training School for the fall quarter, which would begin in September, just a few short weeks away. Within days, I received via e-mail a letter of acceptance.

The Crossroads School was for people over thirty-five who were at a crossroads in their lives and looking for direction. It was a perfect fit for me, but this was August, and I had much to do to be packed and ready to go by September. I was excited! So many questions ran through my mind. Could it be that God was preparing me to be a full-time missionary and live in some foreign country? Was that the plan He had for this new season of my life? Was this the way I would find the happiness and fulfillment I had been longing for? I didn't get answers to any of those questions, but I had a peace inside that this was to be my next step.

With this new vision in front of me, I quickly set to work taking care of all the necessary details. I immediately gave notice to my employer that I would be leaving my position and going to a foreign mission's organization for training. I had a feeling I would not be returning to my job, but just in case, I asked if I could have a leave of absence rather than a formal resignation. They graciously approved.

In September 2009, with all details finalized and everything covered on the home front, I said goodbye to friends and family and boarded a jet for Honolulu. From there I caught a plane to Kona, where I was met by a staff member from the university and shuttled to the campus. After going through all the required checkpoints, I got checked in for classes and received my dorm assignment. I then paid the necessary fees and was escorted to my living quarters, where I would be staying for the duration of my time at Kona.

With my flight from the mainland, the time standing in long lines to complete registration, and more, it had been a very long day, and I was exhausted. Walking into the dorm and seeing the bunk that was reserved for me was a welcomed sight. I quickly pulled sheets and a pillow out of my suitcase and put my bed together for a good night's sleep, but not before getting introduced to some of my roommates and fellow Crossroaders.

As I said my prayers for the night, I thanked God for my being there on this world-renowned missionary training campus. Who would have thought I would ever be there? I also acknowledged His goodness and faithfulness to me. I would tell Him often, "You are better to me than ten earthly husbands, and I am so thankful, so grateful."

The first ten weeks of our training was in a classroom setting there at the university. Each week we would have the privilege of listening to a seasoned missionary tell of his or her experiences in the field. Each speaker had a different anointing or strength, so each week was exciting and filled with stories of God's faithfulness to them in their individual assignments. Some had assignments in the United States or Canada, whereas others had been assigned throughout the world. My favorite was a man who was based out of Colorado, but his assignment was to the Muslim peoples of the earth. He told us stories of being in Turkey with other missionaries and how God had supernaturally given them the language they needed to converse with some men at a local water fountain in order to lead the men to Jesus. We heard many such stories all intended to build our faith and take us to another level of believing.

During the last six weeks of lectures, we were presented with the countries where we would be going for the second part of our training—the outreach part. This is where we would take what we had learned in the classroom and put it into practical use. The Crossroads' students were given two countries to choose from for the outreach portion: India and Cambodia. Right away I dismissed going to Cambodia because I had heard of the Khmer Rouge that had happened there in the mid to late seventies. I had heard news reports on US television of Cambodians getting legs blown off by land mines that still lay under the ground's surface, and I was afraid to go there.

As the countries were presented to us, we were asked to seek God individually as to which country He would have us go to. Once His will was revealed to us, we were to submit an e-mail to the directors of Crossroads indicating the country we had chosen.

I was sure that I should go to India. I had been there on

a mission trip with a group from my church in 1999 and had always thought of going back someday. I was sure this was my opportunity to do just that. Besides, I did not desire to go to Cambodia. Every time I would sit down at the computer to submit my request for India, I would become troubled in my spirit. I did not have peace that India was the country God wanted me to go to. After trying a couple of times to submit my request, I finally called out to God. I repented of being fearful and for not seeking His will for my life. I told Him that if He wanted me to go to Cambodia, I would obey, and I would trust Him to protect me. After all, had He not already brought me through so much? How could I doubt that He would always protect me, no matter where I was and no matter what I faced? I finally was able to submit my request, and great peace accompanied that decision. I knew I was in the center of God's will, right where I was supposed to be.

Now that I knew my assignment, I had another issue facing me. When I had arrived at the school six weeks earlier, I had had enough funds to cover my room and board and the classroom portion of the training. I did not have enough to cover the outreach assignment. The school told me that I had a few weeks to come up with the funds needed, but if I could not, I would not be allowed to go on the outreach. Instead, I would return to my home in California.

I knew that God had brought me to this school, and I knew that He wanted me to go to Cambodia. I had peace that somehow, He would provide everything I needed. I was in peace, and I simply refused to worry about where the funds would come from. After a couple of days, I received an e-mail from my oldest brother and his wife stating that they would be sending me support of a certain sum of money each month. Then a few days later, a couple I had attended church with in California e-mailed me that they would be sending monthly financial support as well. I had an income from my ex-husband's retirement that came into my bank account on a monthly basis. With all these together, I was still short to have the fees for the outreach portion paid in time. I did not let anyone know that I was short on funds. I simply believed that God would provide.

One morning as I was in the common living area of our dormitory, I was addressed by one of the other residents. "Dorothy," she started, "I had a dream about you last night." She went on to say, "In the dream, you and I were both being interviewed by a panel of people. At the end of the interview, they turned to me and said, 'You already have all you need. We will give this to Dorothy.'" She said that they had been referring to money, to funds needed for ministry opportunity. She then asked me if the dream meant anything to me. I told her that it did and that I had been believing God for the rest of the funds I needed to pay for the outreach portion of my training. She finished by saying, "Well, it's on the way." She and I began to joyously dance around the room, thanking God for all the funds needed for the trip to arrive in a timely manner so that I could turn them in at the proper time.

As we were doing so, another one of our roommates walked in and asked why we were celebrating. We told her about the dream and how we believed God would give me all that I needed. She then joined in the celebration and said she would like to donate to the cause. She went to her bunk area and soon returned, handing me a personal check for one hundred dollars. As other roommates heard about the dream, they too began to offer support. When all was said and done, I had received one thousand dollars cash from the others. When the funds from all sources had been added up, I had more than enough to pay my fees for the outreach to Cambodia.

By now, I had no doubt that God wanted me to go to Cambodia, and I wanted to hurry up and get there. As the various teams gathered at the flagpoles to catch our shuttles to the airport, excitement filled the air. I was sure there had been others who, just like me, had believed God for some last-minute provision and saw Him come through in a wonderful way. And now here we were, standing with bags packed and ready to catch our flights to worlds unknown. We didn't know exactly what God had in store for us in the various countries we would all be flying to, but we knew He definitely wanted us to go. When you go with such confidence and surety, you can't help but wonder what He's up to. I asked myself, "What adventures and lessons does He have in store for me in Cambodia?"

3

HE IS COMMITTED TO ME

Don't be obsessed with money but live content with what you have, for you always have God's presence. For hasn't He promised you, "I will never leave you alone, never! And I will not loosen my grip on your life!" So we can say with great confidence: "I know the Lord is for me and I will never be afraid of what people may do to me!"

—HEBREWS 13:5-6 (TPT)

We flew out of Honolulu on the evening of December 16, 2009. After doing an all-night layover in Taipei, Taiwan, and flying four hours to Phnom Penh, and adjusting to the new time zone (which was seventeen hours ahead of Honolulu), we were all ready for a comfortable room in a great hotel. However, that was not what we got. The rooms that had been reserved for us to spend the night on our first evening in Cambodia were very rough with only basic accommodations. There were two metal twin beds and a toilet-shower combination per room. There was nothing comforting at all about the rooms. They were cold and uninviting. I remember wondering how I would ever fall asleep in such surroundings. It felt more like a prison cell than a hotel room. But fall asleep I did—and soundly, I might add.

We rose early the next morning, showered, dressed, and quickly vacated the property. I was thankful for the wonderful night's rest and for the fact that I had a pillow to lay my head on. I had to remind myself that I was in a third-world country now, and things would not be as I was familiar with at home. In such times, I found comfort in knowing that my God had promised to never leave me or forsake me, and that He had already provided all that I would need for each and every day—all that I would need, not all that I might want, even though He sometimes gives us our wants as well.

After a wonderful Cambodian breakfast in a very nice restaurant, we were off to catch a bus that would carry us to our assigned cities. The team I was on consisted of nine people, five singles and two married couples. There was a second team that was comprised mostly of families, and they were assigned to the town of Siem Reap. Our team was assigned to the province of Kampong Thom in the very heart of the nation. When the bus arrived there, the driver simply stopped on the side of the road, opened the door, and let us off. We had no room reservations and did not know where we would stay, but we did have a local citizen as a contact. He was a local businessman and pastor, and he was waiting when the bus arrived. I can still see him now. He was a young, nice-looking Cambodian man, and he wore a bright yellow shirt with a very large Tweety Bird on the front of it, western style trousers and a big smile on his face. He was a most welcome sight.

After much deliberation between this man and the two leaders of our team, it was decided that we should stay in a small hotel in the main part of town. It was a little noisy at times but safe and definitely affordable.

During our six-week stay in Kampong Thom, we were given many opportunities to minister publicly and share the gospel. The local World Vision office located there had asked our staff team leader if one of us would be willing to bring the gospel at their Christmas party. The party was not only for their staff but also many city officials who had been invited. I volunteered to bring the message. What a blessing it was to minister to so many in that setting.

We also taught English as a second language in villages

throughout the province. On New Year's Eve, our pastor friend hosted a celebration at his church, and many whom we had been ministering to came and gave their hearts to Jesus. The next day, they were baptized in a nearby lake.

I could go on and on about the details of the exciting adventure we were on with our Lord. We attended church services in villages where we were allowed to bring the gospel message through Bible stories and through skits, and many came to the Lord. Our team put on a five-day Bible school for the employees at the World Vision office, and four of the young men working there gave their lives to Jesus. Some of us went to an AIDS hospital and prayed with the women patients. We ministered at an orphanage that not only housed abandoned children but also took in girls that had been rescued from sex trafficking. God's goodness and grace were ever present with us. We would discover special little treats such as ice cream from South Korea or yogurts from Europe, and as we indulged in the goodies, we knew God was giving us a taste of home. We knew it was His special way of letting us know how personally He cares for each one of us.

These were some of the really great things we got to take part in, but there were other things that we saw that were not so wonderful. We saw things like extreme poverty, child abuse and abandonment, adults blinded or maimed by land mines, parents to care for their children with little to no assistance, bodies riddled with disease and infirmity, and others dying for lack of medical attention following an automobile accident. These are things that get to you after a while.

I know that Jesus paid for all sickness, disease, poverty, and lack at Calvary. In Mark 16:17–18 (NKJV), Jesus says,

> And these signs will follow those who believe;
> In My name they will cast out demons; they
> will speak with new tongues; they will take up
> serpents; and if they drink anything deadly,
> it will by no means hurt them; they will lay
> hands on the sick, and they will recover.

I know that as born-again believers who have the spirit of almighty God living on the inside, we carry the solution to every foul thing that Satan unleashes on the earth. Whether or not those people know our God doesn't really matter. We know Him, and we should be releasing our faith and making Him and all His goodness known as we go throughout the earth. That's what Jesus did, and He is our example. Acts 10:38 (NKJV) says it this way:

> How God anointed Jesus of Nazareth with
> the Holy Spirit and with power, who went
> about doing good and healing all who were
> oppressed by the devil, for God was with Him.

I was very familiar with these scriptures, and others, that tell us the authority that has been given to us as believers and followers of Christ. Yet we weren't seeing a lot of the miraculous happen as we prayed for people. Didn't Mark 16:17, which I referenced earlier, state these signs will follow those who believe? Well, I for one was a believer, so where were the signs? I came to one conclusion: either I didn't really believe what the Bible said on the subject, or I didn't understand how to release faith to see it manifest. Convinced that it was the latter, I began to ask the Lord to teach me about faith and how it works.

Upon completion of the outreach portion of our missionary training, we flew back to Kona for debriefing. After that, we all headed back to our respective homes. I continued to go on short-term mission trips as opportunities became available. In the fall of 2010, I went back to Nepal for my third time, and in the spring of 2011, I went to Nairobi, Kenya, for my first time. The trips were always wonderful, and I'm very thankful for the doors that were open for me to teach and share the gospel where ever I went. However, I always came home feeling a little disappointed because I had not seen blind eyes opened or the lame made to dance. I was so hungry to see the miraculous manifested, as Jesus had promised it would when the gospel is preached. My constant prayer was, "Lord, teach me about faith and how to release it."

On Mother's Day 2011, my youngest son suggested to me that I should relocate from California to Fort Worth, Texas, where he and his family were residing at the time. I agreed to visit them in June of that year and see what the Lord would show me concerning a move. I had already decided that I no longer wanted to work a secular job. I told the Lord that if it were okay with Him, I would really enjoy working for a ministry. I knew there were several well-known ministries in the Dallas–Fort Worth area, and it would be no difficult matter for the Lord to open the right door for me.

I went online and submitted my resume to a few of the larger ministries with current openings that were within twenty miles of my son's home. Within a few days, I received a call from one such ministry, which set appointments to get me started with the interview and testing process. Once I successfully completed the process, they offered me a position on the phone lines of their customer service department, which I was thrilled to accept. I went back to California, got my affairs in order, packed what I could carry in my car, and relocated to Fort Worth. I stayed with my son and his family until I could find suitable housing for myself.

I started my new position on October 6, 2011. Once again, I was in a place that I had never, in my wildest imaginations, dreamed I would be. This ministry had a daily television program where they taught on the topic of faith straight from the Word of God. While I was going through the interview process, the Lord had told me that I would be offered a position with them. He told me that He was sending me to school to learn about faith, but this time He was going to pay me to learn. It was more than I could fathom. I was overwhelmed as I realized just how much He is committed to me, and as He says in His word,

Ask, and it will be given to you; seek, and you will find; knock, and it will be opened to you. (Mathew 7:7 NKJV)

I found myself saying yet again, "God, You are better to me than ten earthly husbands, and I love You so much."

4

I WAS CREATED BY DESIGN AND FOR A PURPOSE

> *You saw who you created me to be before I became me! Before I'd ever seen the light of day, the number of days you planned for me were already recorded in your book.*
>
> —PSALM 139:16 (TPT)

When I read Psalm 139, I become very aware that almighty God, Creator of the universe and everything in it, knows me by name. He knew me before I was ever born. He has a plan and a purpose for my life and for everyone's life, and those plans are written in books kept in heaven. His plans are for good, not for evil (Jeremiah 29:11). But He has also given us a free will, and we can choose to follow His plan or make our own plans. He does not desire for us to be His robots and love Him because He commands us to. Rather, He wants us to love Him because we choose to.

I must admit there have been times in my life when I was following His plan for me, and there were times when I was doing my own thing and following my own plan. It was in those times of self-will and stubbornness that I made decisions and took actions that eventually delivered me into some dark places in my life. It was the natural result or the outworking of those poor choices. But thank God that He never left me to walk through it alone. Psalm 139:11 (TPT) says it this way:

> It's impossible to disappear from you or to ask
> the darkness to hide me, for your presence
> is everywhere, bringing light into my night.
> There is no such thing as darkness with you.
> The night, to you, is as bright as the day;
> there's no difference between the two.

How comforting those words have been in times when I felt all hope was gone. When darkness surrounded me and I couldn't feel His presence or hear His gentle voice leading me, I simply had to trust what I read in the Bible to be the truth about my situation. The Bible says that "we are more than conquerors" (Romans 8:37) whether or not we feel like it. It says, "The Lord is near to the brokenhearted and saves those who are crushed in spirit" (Psalm 34:18 NASB), even if it doesn't feel like He's near. The promises go on and on. We simply have to believe they are true. We believe by faith, not by feelings.

It's similar to flying an airplane. I am not a pilot, and I have never even been in the cockpit of a plane, but I have heard experts say that when pilots are flying through thick fog, they have to trust their instrument panel to know what to do. They may feel like they are flying right side up when actually they are flying upside down. In the fog, you can't tell the difference because you can't see the horizon. Many pilots have crashed their planes into the ocean depths or the side of a mountain simply because they chose to believe their feelings over the plane's instrument readings. This error in judgment led to their own deaths as well as the deaths of friends and family members who were flying with them.

When I hear of such tragic events, my mind tends to go to the lives of Christians. How many times do we trust our feelings over what the Bible has to say concerning our situation? The Apostle Paul addresses it when he is instructing Timothy.

Holding on to faith and a good conscience, which some have rejected and so have suffered shipwreck with regard to the faith. (1 Timothy 1:19 NIV)

When we disregard the teachings of our Lord and allow our own feelings to dictate to us, we become shipwrecked in our faith. If we don't quickly repent and get in line with the Word, we can cause those close to us to become shipwrecked as well.

I have been guilty of this very thing. For example, after my divorce, the enemy bombarded my mind with accusing thoughts about God. He wanted me to believe that God had betrayed me and that He was not fair or just. I had walked with my Lord for a very long time, and He was always faithful to me. I knew Satan's accusations against God were not true, but he kept relentlessly hammering my mind and would even present situations as evidence to confirm his accusations. I began to find myself having trust issues with God and everyone else. I started feeling that if anything good was going to happen in my life, I would have to make it happen. No one, not even God, was going to do it for me. Then one morning, the Lord led me to a verse in the Bible.

He is the Rock, His works are perfect, and all His ways are just. A faithful God who does no wrong, upright and just is He. (Deuteronomy 32:4 NIV)

As I read that verse, I could either choose to believe it or choose to believe the lie of the enemy. I quickly repented for doubting God's goodness. I then memorized this verse and used it as a weapon against the enemy of my soul. Every time he shot his fiery arrows into my mind, I countered his lies with the truth. I spent no time arguing with Satan or trying to belittle him. I simply opened my mouth and spoke the Word. It didn't take long for that harassment to stop once I put the truth on it. Satan hates hearing the truth. I have learned that is the quickest way to get rid of him, and that is also a promise of God.

> Submit yourselves therefore to God. Resist
> the devil, and he will flee from you. (James
> 4:7 KJV)

When I moved to Fort Worth, the Lord connected me with some very strong women of prayer. The first connection was with a woman outside of work. I was attending church with her at that time. She was very anointed not only in prayer but also in the prophetic. I would often receive encouragement from her through the ministry gifts that flowed from her, and we became good friends. She held a prayer group in her home with some of the other ladies from that church. We would meet at her house for prayer a couple of times a month. These ladies were strong prayers, and as I spent time with them, my prayer life went to a new level. I had always been a strong prayer and believed in the power of prayer, but there was still much I needed to learn on the subject. God was surrounding me with people from whom I could learn. I've heard it said that prayer is more often caught than taught. Simply get into a healthy prayer environment, and your prayer life will take on new dimensions. That has certainly held true in my life.

After working at the ministry for three years, I was transferred from customer service phone lines to the prayer phone lines. It was the policy of the ministry that we would pray only the Word. In doing so, we knew we were praying the will of God because His Word is His will. For every situation we may walk through in life, there is a Bible verse that promises victory. The Holy Spirit would direct us to that promise, and we would pray it over the particular situation with the caller. We would receive so many testimonies of how our partners saw victory once the Word of God was released in faith. In praying this way, I also received the benefit of committing to memory many of the promises of God.

There, at the ministry, the Lord blessed me with some friendships that are still with me today. These ladies had been on the prayer phone lines for a very long time and had developed a deep place of prayer in their personal lives as a result. I learned much about prayer from them.

By now, God had asked me to move from the smaller church I had been attending to a larger church that was part of the ministry where I had been working. Prayer was a big part of this new church, and I was given even more opportunities to learn and grow. At one point, I was asked to lead a prayer group focused on praying for families of the church. I accepted the challenge, and even though it was unfamiliar territory for me, the Lord was gracious to me. By His grace, I am growing into a prayer-group leader.

I no longer live in Texas, and I no longer pray with those ladies on a regular basis, but the Lord continues to give me opportunities to develop my prayer life. I don't yet see how this new place in prayer fits into the divine scheme of things or His will and plan for my life, but I know that it does. He moved me halfway across the United States, gave me a position on the phone lines of a worldwide television ministry, and surrounded me with strong and mature intercessors on every side so I could come up higher in my prayer life and learn more about faith. Yes, indeed, I think He has a plan for me that includes living by faith, not by sight, and praying on another level. If you are going to live by faith, a strong prayer life is a must!

That is His will for all of us. He doesn't want any of us to remain as we are but to always be growing in the things of God. He will bring opportunities to us for growth, but it is up to us to accept them. Those opportunities always include challenges. Many want the growth but not the challenge, so they decline the opportunity. The sad thing is they don't realize they can't have one without the other. Consequently, they remain as they are year after year, and the Christian life becomes boring to them. Our lives in Jesus should be anything but boring.

One of the great things about our God is the fact that He

never gives up on us, and He doesn't mark us as failures if we don't pass the test the first time. He gives us the opportunity to go through the test over and over again until we pass, no matter how long it takes. If we refuse to take the test, it doesn't simply go away. The opportunity will come to us again until we finally accept the challenge. It's the only way we can grow, and He is committed to our spiritual growth.

As I walk with the Lord, I have learned that I am not defined by my circumstances, my failures, or my successes. People cannot tell me who I am, only God. He is the one who created me, and I am not an accident or simply the result of my mom and dad's passion. I am here on planet Earth because Creator God has deemed it to be so. It's that plain and that simple.

> Even before we were born, God planned in advance our destiny and the good works we would do to fulfill it. (Ephesians 2:10b TPT)

God created us with a specific purpose in mind: to complete an assignment. When He formed us in our mothers' wombs, He placed within us everything we would need in order to succeed in that assignment. Our height, our build, the color of our hair and eyes, our level of intelligence, where we would be born, to whom we would be born—all these things he considered as He framed us in the womb, and all of it is for His plans and purposes.

First and foremost, we were created to have fellowship

with God. This is our divine purpose. In case you have ever wondered why you are here, this is why. We can see that as we look at the story of the creation of humans in Genesis. God was accustomed to walking and talking with Adam and Eve in the garden in the cool of the day.

> And they heard the sound of the Lord God walking in the garden in the cool of the day, and Adam and his wife hid themselves from the presence of the Lord God among the trees of the garden. (Genesis 3:8 NKJV)

The word translated as *walking* in this verse refers to repetitive and habitual movement, so this happened on a regular basis, and they were familiar with it. It wasn't new or strange to them. Also, Psalm 8:4 (NKJV) states, "What is man that You are mindful of him, and the son of man that You visit him?"

We see from Genesis that God created Adam and Eve and gave them assignments. He also fellowshipped with them daily and gave them instructions concerning those assignments. When they failed through disobedience, He didn't destroy them. Instead, He made a way to forgive that sin. In the Old Testament, because Jesus had not yet died on the cross, animal sacrifices were used as the method of atonement for sin, looking forward to the coming Messiah who would make an end to animal sacrifice. In the New Testament, Jesus was that perfect sacrifice for all sin. John the Baptist proclaimed it in John 1:29 (ESV) when he said, "Behold the Lamb of God who takes away the sin of the world."

In order for us to complete our God-given assignments here on Earth, we must first believe that Jesus did indeed make atonement for our sins at the cross of Calvary. When we acknowledge that and receive Jesus as our Savior, our sins are washed away, and we become righteous before God.

> For He made Him who knew no sin to be sin
> for us, that we might become the righteousness
> of God in Him. (2 Corinthians 5:21 NKJV)

We see from this verse that there is actually an exchange that takes place: Jesus takes our sin and gives us His righteousness. Once that happens, we are restored to a place of unbroken relationship with our Creator, God, just as it was in the garden of Eden before Adam sinned. Along with this new birth experience, we become citizens of the kingdom of heaven. Now we can walk with God and talk with Him. His Holy Spirit takes up residence on the inside of us, and He will guide us into all truth and show us things that are to come (John 16:13 KJV). He teaches us how to live and how to operate according to kingdom principles. God takes us into our destinies by the leading of the Holy Spirit, but we must learn to be sensitive to His promptings and be willing to obey.

As we walk in our destinies, we find fulfillment in life,

but this is not where we find our identities. We are first and foremost children of God, and He is pleased with us not because of anything we do but because of what Jesus did on our behalf.

After my divorce, I went through an identity crisis. For thirty-seven years, I had found my identity in being a wife and a mother. Then all of a sudden, I was no longer active in those roles. I didn't know who I was or what I was supposed to do. I got very depressed. Then I learned that my identity is not in what I do or what title people may put on me; my identity is found in Christ alone. That is not based on anything that I did to earn it; it's based on what Jesus did for me. I had head knowledge of these truths prior to my divorce, but I had no revelation of what it really meant. Consequently, I did not live according to that knowledge. Suddenly, I realized that if I were going to continue to live and have healthy emotions and relationships, I was going to have to learn how to apply that knowledge and start seeing myself the way God sees me. Jesus's sinless blood has washed all my sins away, and I have acknowledged before Him that I believe God sees me as His child and loves me as much as He does Jesus. That is really good news, and it takes all pressure off me to perform for His love and acceptance; I've already got it, even if I never accomplish anything for Him.

Actually, the best thing any of us could ever do for Him is to humble ourselves before Him, acknowledging He is God and we are not. As we submit our will to His will, yielding to the promptings and leadings of the Holy Spirit from within our spirit, we will find ourselves living in that place of intimacy with the Father, walking in unbroken fellowship with Him. To have a humble heart is the only way true intimacy with Him can be obtained. The following quote from Andrew Murray says it very well.

> The highest glory of the creature is in being only a vessel, to receive and enjoy and show forth the glory of God. It can do this only as it is willing to be nothing in itself, that God may be all. Water always fills first the lowest places. The lower, the emptier a man lies before God, the speedier and the fuller will be the inflow of the divine glory.[2]

I hunger for this kind of selflessness—to be so dead to self and selfish ambitions that I can reflect His glory to a lost world that desperately needs to see Him. The cry of my heart is, "Oh, Lord, teach me to humble myself. Help me to receive every offense that comes my way as a blessed opportunity to respond in love, and to remain silent if necessary, thereby crucifying my flesh and becoming a vessel You can use."

---

[2] "Quotes by Andrew Murray," https://www.goodreads.com, taken from the book *Humility: The Journey Toward Holiness*.

5

NO WEAPON FORMED WILL PROSPER

"No weapon formed against you shall prosper, and every tongue which rises against you in judgment you shall condemn. This is the heritage of the servants of the Lord, and their righteousness is from Me," Says the Lord.

—ISAIAH 54:17 (NKJV)

In the days and months following my separation from my husband, people began to talk about the situation. Everyone had an opinion as to what had really happened in our relationship: a marriage of thirty-six years that had seemed on the surface to be so healthy and strong. Some of the comments that made their way back to me were laughable; others were cruel and hurtful.

When people don't know what has actually taken place, they begin to make assumptions. They may know some of the details, and based on what they know, they fill in the blanks. No one knows the whole truth except the people who are actually walking through it.

During this time, the devil was working overtime trying to destroy me, or at least make me quit and give up in my walk with the Lord. I was constantly battling negative thoughts in my mind about myself and how hopeless my life had become. I was never suicidal, but there were days when I would tell the Lord that if He wanted to take me on to heaven, I would be okay with it. Then I heard the comments being made, and the things I was being accused of that were so far from the truth that I would have laughed at had it not been so painful.

From every side, I was being accused of things that weren't even in my character to do, and oh, how that hurt! As painful as my divorce was, this was a close second in emotional pain.

I constantly looked to the truth and the promises of the Word of God to give me the strength and courage to continue. The verse I referenced at the beginning of this chapter was always an encouragement to me. I knew that even though the weapon had been formed against me, it would not prosper. I also knew that somehow God would vindicate me of the character assassination. I had to keep my eyes on Him and not try to vindicate myself. I also knew that I needed to come to a place within me where people's opinions no longer mattered, and the only opinion I cared about was God's. In John 5:44 (NASB), Jesus said, "How can you believe, when you receive glory from one another and you do not seek the glory that is from the one and only God?"

In other words, we should care only about receiving approval from God and not from people. If we can truly come to the place where we give no attention to the praises of others, then we will no longer care about their criticisms either. That trap of performance to win the approval of others will be broken forever, and their negative opinions of us will no longer turn our world upside down. It simply won't matter to us any longer.

Another lesson I learned during this time was to love my enemies, bless those who were cursing me, do good to those who hated me, and pray for those who were spitefully using me and persecuting me (Matthew 5:44 NKJV). I began to execute this command as best I could, praying fervently for the Lord's grace and wisdom as I prayed for each one by name. Every time the enemy brought a hurtful thought to my mind concerning what someone had said or done against me, I would stop what I was doing and pray for that person. I would ask the Lord to give the person revelation of truth anywhere he or she was believing error, and I would ask Him to bless the person's life. This brought a quick end to the devil's harassment because it was backfiring on him. He didn't want me to bless my enemies—he wanted me to hate them and become bitter. That way, I would never fulfill the call of God on my life. Because I chose to walk in obedience to God's Word, it opened a door for the Lord to vindicate me on all levels. I experienced the peace of God and His blessings on my life like never before.

Of course, the enemy of my soul never gives up. He tries continually to get me to take offense at one thing or another, but now I know what to do. I pray for those people at the first sign of irritation, and when possible, I like to meet with them and talk it out, or give them a gift of some kind as an act of honoring and blessing them. I'm not saying I have perfected this in my life. It will take me a lifetime of walking it out, I'm sure, but when our desire is to obey God, He meets us in that place and gives us His grace for the situation, and then it becomes easier to do.

I am highly motivated to learn to walk in love toward all people, but especially those who wrong me. It's what Jesus did, and He is our example. I do not want to live the remainder of my years a bitter, unforgiving old woman with a victim mentality. Therefore, I look to Jesus's example and ask Him to teach me to love as He loves.

One morning, while I was in my prayer time, I caught a

vision of Jesus on the cross. He allowed me to see through His eyes, and I saw His eyes looking not just at those at the foot of the cross but across the entire crowd of people standing there. They were mocking Him, pointing and jeering, spitting at Him, and speaking blasphemies, and with His heart of compassion and mercy, He forgave. He was more concerned about their lost condition than the pain and rejection He was suffering. He gladly became their Savior and ours. He willingly went to that cross to pay for every sin that had ever been or ever would be committed. All we have to do is believe and receive it for ourselves. While still hanging on the cross, He looked at the ones who nailed Him there and prayed for them: "Father, forgive them; for they know not what they do" (Luke 23:24 KJV).

I have never suffered anything that would even come close to the betrayal or physical and emotional pain that Jesus suffered for me. If He can forgive like that, then I can forgive the petty little things that have happened to me.

> For our light affliction, which is but for a moment, is working for us a far more exceeding and eternal weight of glory, while we do not look at the things which are seen, but at the things which are not seen. For the things which are seen are temporary, but the things which are not seen are eternal. (2 Corinthians 4:17–18 NKJV)

DOROTHY PINO

Everything we see here on this earth is temporary and will eventually fade away, and someday our eyes will behold Jesus, our Savior. When we see His beautiful face, we will be so glad that we kept the faith, that we loved hard and forgave quickly, and that we had our treasure in heaven and not in the temporal things of this earth.

As I mentioned earlier, I had asked the Lord to teach me to love the way He loves, and He gave me an opportunity to walk that out.

On the morning of November 15, 2016, I received a call from my daughter, Perri, who lived near her dad in California. She was obviously upset and in tears. Perri informed me that her father, my ex-husband, had suffered a stroke sometime during the night; they were not sure what time. His landlord had called to let her know that James had been taken by ambulance to St. Mary's Hospital in Apple Valley and that he was in critical condition. I was shocked. We all were. No one was expecting this. We all knew that James had some health issues and was taking several medications, but he seemed to have it all under control. He had played eighteen holes of golf with a close friend a week prior, and the day before the stroke, he had taken our daughter and son-in-law, Ray, to dinner for their birthdays. Before they went to the restaurant, they stopped by our oldest grandson's home because James wanted to pray with him and his girlfriend. Ray told me later that it was the most powerful prayer he had ever heard. We knew that the enemy was coming against James's health because of the anointing he carried. We refused to fear. We stayed optimistic for his speedy recovery.

As the family began to gather at the hospital and listen to the prognosis from his doctor, we realized that James was not expected to recover. They gave us one bad report after another, but we couldn't give up on him. Our entire family would fill his room daily and speak words of encouragement to him. Our oldest granddaughter, Whitley, bought him a quilt, wrote healing scriptures from the Bible all over it, and laid it over him. One of our grandsons, Tyler, is a barber, and he would come in and give his grandpa a shave and make sure his hair was well groomed. Other children and grandchildren would bring him his favorite foods each day, once he was able to eat again. We rallied around him and poured our love and prayers over him, not to mention his siblings and friends who would come see him daily and love on him. He had no lack of affection shown to him.

James tried as best he could to respond, but his body had been so weakened by the stroke. His heart was only functioning at about 20 percent; he was paralyzed on the right side and had lost his ability to speak and to swallow. He would nod his head for yes or shake it for no, and this was how he communicated with us. He seemed to be able to comprehend our conversations for the most part, and sometimes he would look so deeply into our eyes as though he wanted to tell us something. I had never thought this would happen to him.

After a few days, James seemed to be making a turn for the better. He had regained his ability to swallow and was now eating some soft foods. My sons and I returned to our homes and our jobs. Perri and her children were the only ones left in California to look after James. He completed five days in the hospital and then was moved to a rehab facility for twenty-one days.

The Lord had been speaking to my heart and asking me if I would like to move to California and care for James once he was released from rehab. While James and I were married, I had looked forward to our golden years with joy. We would be retired, and life would be at a slower pace, with more time for traveling and spending time with our children and grandchildren. Then the divorce happened, and although I had always hoped deep inside that our marriage would someday be restored, I hadn't spent much time thinking of what our physical health would be like should the restoration take place. Now here I was, face-to-face with a question from God and no promise that James would recover. Perri had already said that she would quit her job and care for her dad in her own home, but I felt that would not be the best thing for either her or her dad. However, the decision was not mine to make because James and I were divorced. Our children would be the ones making the final decisions concerning their father's health and well-being. I suggested to them that I would be willing to quit my job and move to California to help with their dad's care. I would watch him during the days while Perri worked, and then she could relieve me some in the evening to rest. This arrangement was agreeable to all three of our children.

When I returned to Fort Worth and to my job at the ministry, I gave notice that my last day of work would be November 30, and of course my resignation was accepted. I gave notice to my landlord that I would be leaving and began to put all my affairs in order, packing what I would be taking with me and putting all else in storage. On December 1, I loaded my car and set out for California along with my Texas daughter-in-law, Janice, who went with me so that I would not have to travel alone.

When the Lord presented to me the opportunity to return to California and care for my husband, I was amazed at how fully and completely I had forgiven him. I had no resentment toward him or anymore feelings of betrayal. As a matter of fact, when I visited him in the hospital and saw him lying there so helpless, my heart was moved with compassion for him. All his life, he had been such a strong, athletic man, and now all his strength was gone. He was at the mercy of others to take care of his every need, and I knew that this had to be very hard on his ego. The bitterness I once felt toward him was gone, and I truly wanted to help him. I was sure that God was going to totally heal James, and our marriage would be restored. I just knew that was what God was up to in all this. As a matter of fact, when I responded to God and told Him that I would like to care for James, I knew that I heard in my heart these very words: "This will be your restoration with him." Putting my own interpretation on what God meant by that, I became so excited.

When James was moved to the rehab facility, they instructed us that once James was home, we would need to get him out of bed each day and provide him with the means to sit up in a chair. They said if he remained in bed too long, he would get bedsores and other complications. My daughter and I began to try to lift him out of bed into a wheelchair there at the rehab, but we could not lift him. He was unable to help support himself, so it was like lifting dead weight. We knew that other arrangements would need to be made, at least for a little while until he could get strong enough to help us move his body weight. On December 13, he was moved from the rehab facility to a privately owned assisted living home there in Apple Valley. I believe James was very disappointed that we didn't take him home with us. I explained to him that as soon as we could learn how to move him from his bed to a chair, we would take him home. He seemed to understand, but his health began to decline.

On the morning of December 16, I received a call from the owner and director of the assisted living home. He informed me that James had stopped breathing and asked me if we wanted him to call 911. I asked him to please call them. I would inform my daughter, and she would meet them at the hospital. Perri was on her way to work when I reached her by phone. This was her first week back since her dad's illness. She immediately jumped on the freeway and headed to the hospital emergency room some thirty miles away. I got dressed and headed to the hospital within twenty minutes. When I arrived at the emergency room, the clerk called to the back and informed my daughter that I was waiting out front. She came out to take me back where her dad was, and with tears streaming down her cheeks she said, "Mom, Dad is gone." She then gave me the details of how the medics had tried in vain to revive her father until she finally told them to stop because he was not responding.

I couldn't believe what I was hearing. I told her that she must be mistaken. As she led me back behind the curtain where James was lying, I could clearly see that he was indeed gone. There was no sign of life in him. I cried out loud to the Lord, "No! You promised me!" Then all of a sudden, I felt the peace of God wrap around me like a warm blanket. I had never felt anything like it ever before. Peace settled in on me, and my emotions felt numb. I couldn't even cry anymore, I just sat there.

I began to question myself and all the events that had transpired over the past few weeks. Did God really ask me to quit my job and come to California for it to end like this? I had only been there two weeks! Had I really heard God at all, or was I simply imagining things in my head? What was this all about, really? How could God get any glory out of such a loss? Without our marriage, and ultimately our family restored, where was the victory? Was it the voice of God I had been following, or the voice of the enemy? I was so hurt and confused. Just like ten years prior, when I had been going through my divorce, the devil started to bombard my mind with thoughts that God couldn't be trusted. Oh, the torment in my mind! Once again, I went back to the truth of the Word of God and stood on what I knew to be true about God. At least this time I had five years of working in a strong faith and strong prayer environment, and I had much ammunition against the devil. It didn't take long this time to silence the avenger and those accusing thoughts about God.

We buried James on December 22, 2016, and all my hopes and dreams of a restored marriage were buried with him. The children prepared a lovely funeral service for their father. He would have been very proud of each one of them and the grandchildren. I know I sure was.

I was still very numb in my emotions at the service and for a long time afterward. I continued to question what had just happened. What had I missed? Was there something I could have done that I didn't do? I felt so foolish that I had believed for ten years my marriage would be restored someday. I felt foolish for having believed it so strongly that I quit a great job and went to care for a man who would have never done the same for me. Then I noticed I was getting bitter and resentful again. I guess unanswered questions can make us that way if we're not careful, but I had already decided that I was not going to live the remainder of my years as a bitter old woman, so I began to ask the Lord to help me understand, and He did.

The Lord began to answer some of my questions. He assured me that there is nothing foolish about being so committed to your marriage that you won't give up on it even when all hope is gone. The Bible says, "Love bears all things, believes all things, hopes all things, endures all things. Love never fails" (1 Corinthians 13:7–8a NKJV).

A couple of months after James had gone on to heaven, I was talking to a friend on the phone. She asked me what had transpired between James and me during those last days that we had together. I told her that although God had not done it the way I thought He would, He did restore us. Our relationship was made whole again, and people around us could see love and a mutual respect between us and commented on it. After I got off the phone with my friend, the Lord plainly asked me a question. I don't mean that I heard a voice, but I heard these words rise up in my spirit: "Do you think I did less for you than what you were believing for?" I didn't want to answer that question because He already knew my heart, and I knew that I must not be correctly seeing the situation. As I was pondering the question and what my answer would be, revelation came to me, and I saw it clearly. Suddenly, I realized that it was a far better thing that God had done for both James and me than what I had been hoping for. What I wanted to see happen was totally selfish on my part. What God did for us brought life and freedom to both James and me. James is more alive now than he has ever been—no more sickness, no more pain, and I am finally free to move on to the next chapter of my life.

I wish I could tell you that this revelation caused me to instantly let go of all bitterness and resentment, but that would not be true. That has been a work in progress, but I think I am finally getting free. I say that because although those negative thoughts come from time to time, I can now quickly recognize them as the work of the devil and refuse to allow them to stay in my mind. Instead, I count my blessings and focus on the promises of God, and before long I see that the negative thoughts are replaced with positive ones.

Heartache and disappointment come to all of us at one time or another in this life. No one is immune to them, but we get to decide how we will respond. Our response will determine our outcome. If we see ourselves as victims, then that's what we will be, but if we see ourselves as overcomers and conquerors, the victory will be sure. The Bible instructs us, "Do not be afraid of sudden terror, nor of trouble from the wicked when it comes; for the Lord will be your confidence, and will keep your foot from being caught" (Proverbs 3:25–26 NKJV).

This verse tells us that when—not if—trouble comes, we are not to fear. Instead, we can rest confidently in the Lord and watch as the enemy is defeated. We do have a part to play, such as stay in faith and stand on the promises of God from His Word, but the battle belongs to the Lord. If we can truly get hold of that revelation, we can stay in peace even when everything is falling apart around us. The closer we get to the return of our Lord, the darker the world will get around us. We must learn how to rest in Him in the middle of trials and stand on the promises of His Word. We might as well practice now so that we can be stronger and wiser for the days ahead.

6

HE IS MY PROVIDER

And my God will supply all your need according to His riches in glory by Christ Jesus.

—PHILIPPIANS 4:19 (NKJV)

As I look back over my life, I stand amazed at the goodness and faithfulness of my God. I see throughout the years His providential hand leading and guiding me all the way, just like a loving father gently leading his child. I know that much of that time I gave no thought to His watchful eye, but all the while He was giving great thought to me and to the specific needs of our family.

One such time was in September 1987. At the age of forty, James had a heart attack while playing a softball game for our church team during a city league game. I had not noticed, but in the middle of the game, he had gone to his truck and laid down in the back. When the game was over, my son James, who had also been playing in the game, came to where I was sitting with some friends and expressed to me that he was concerned about his father. He informed me that his dad had left the game and was lying down. I had been so busy visiting with the ladies, and none of us had noticed this turn of events. I quickly went to James and asked if he needed to go to the hospital. He assured me he was okay; he even wanted to drive home. As we drove toward home, I convinced him that maybe he should go to the emergency room at the hospital to get checked out and make sure there were no problems.

Upon arriving at the ER and telling them his symptoms, they immediately took him back to be examined by a doctor. They informed me that the EKG showed some irregularities, and they would be keeping James overnight for observation. They said I would probably be able to pick him up the next morning, but that did not happen. Early the next morning, James called me and said that apparently he had suffered a mild heart attack. I was quickly dressed and at the hospital to speak with the attending physician, who happened to be a respected cardiologist in our town. The doctor spoke with James and me and said they were still waiting for some test results, but they would keep us informed as they gathered the information. They kept a watch on his condition for a couple of days. Then two days after he had been admitted to the hospital, his doctor came to me with his conclusions. He gave me so many facts and numbers, and though I didn't totally understand the information, I knew it was not good. The hospital James was in was very small and not equipped to handle the situation should his condition worsen, and the doctor seemed to think that was a very real possibility. He suggested that we transport James via helicopter to Loma Linda University Medical Center, approximately one hour away. I approved, and the doctor made all the arrangements. Within a couple of hours, James was in flight to Loma Linda, and they were waiting to receive him into their cardiac care unit. This new hospital was much larger than the one in our hometown, and James received a much higher level of care. He was able to relax, and his condition began to get better. Over the next thirty days, some in the hospital and some as outpatient, there were more tests ordered, including an angiogram. The results showed that out of the five major arteries in his heart, one was totally occluded, the best one was 90 percent occluded, and the other three were somewhere

DOROTHY PINO

in between. The conclusion was that James would need to undergo heart bypass surgery. The surgery was set for the next morning.

I knew that following the surgery, James would need to be off work for several months—if he was able to return at all. He had already been off for a month, and I hadn't worked outside the home for a couple of years. However, I was not worried because just two weeks prior to his heart attack, provision had been put in place for this. James had sold a piece of commercial property that we had purchased seven years prior. He had sold the land and carried back the trust deed so the monthly payments were coming to us. We had partners in the deal that received 49 percent of the interest, and we retained 51 percent. The monthly income was divided accordingly. Our 51 percent of the total payment each month was greater income than what James had been earning while he was working. God knew that at that exact moment in time we would need an income, so He moved on James's heart seven years prior to purchase the land, giving it enough time to appreciate sufficiently in value to provide for our needs. I could tell you several such stories, but none are as grand as this one. Well, there is one other that is just as grand, and it concerns provision for my retirement.

When James had prepared his paperwork for retirement from the Teamsters Union, he requested survivor's benefits to be paid to me should he pass away before me. Also, after the divorce, he advised me that when it came time for me to file for my social security benefits, I should file as his ex-wife.

He said it would bring a greater benefit payment to me over the years. I did as he said but wasn't really aware of how great the benefit would be until he passed away. Through these two acts, God provided, through my husband, an income that will last for the remainder of my life. When I quit my job in Texas to go care for him, I knew this provision was in place, but I didn't know exactly what the amount would be. I didn't give it any thought. I knew that if God wanted me to go, He would provide all I would need. He promises that in His Word, and he had always been faithful to me, so I wasn't concerned.

Now, I see why God had asked me to quit my job and go be restored to James. He knew that James would not be on this earth much longer and that I would no longer need to work for an income. For me to leave my place of employment and be reconciled to my husband was the most important thing to do. All else had already been taken care of.

I could go on and on with stories of the wonderful ways that God has supernaturally provided for me. Like the house that He allowed me to purchase in Texas and then sell twenty-four months later, doubling the cash investment I had made in the home as a down payment. Then I relocated to California, and the Lord had blessed my sister with two houses full of furniture so she was able to totally furnish a two-bedroom apartment for me. Because I didn't need to move things from Texas, I was able to bless several people with some very nice things that they needed.

I grew up in a Christian home and was taught about

tithing and that if you honor God with your finances, you will have His supernatural provision over your life (Malachi 3:10–11). I have been a tither for many years. James had allowed me to tithe even before he gave his life to the Lord. We were tithers because we knew it was the right thing to do. After walking through some very challenging situations in my life and knowing that it's only by God's grace and providential care that I made it through, I can now say as Job did: "I have heard of You by the hearing of the ear, but now my eye sees You" (Job 42:5 NKJV)

Job wasn't just referring to the area of finances here. He was talking about how he had come to know God for himself as he walked through the trouble that had come upon him. It can be that way for anyone. If we will look for Him in the midst of the storm, we will find Him there. He is the stillness, the peace that is guiding us through. Sometimes it's just a knowing inside to go this way or stay here for a while; however, in the end, we will see that it was Him. What a loving Father we have.

> For God has proved His love by giving us His
> greatest treasure, the gift of His son. And since
> God freely offered Him up as the sacrifice for us
> all, He certainly won't withhold from us anything
> else He has to give. (Romans 8:31 TPT)

All we have need of, He has already provided. All we have to do is ask in faith, believing that what He has promised, He will do.

7

THE DIVINE ROMANCE

The one I love calls to me: Arise, my dearest.
Hurry, my darling. Come away with me!

I have come as you have asked to draw you to my heart
and lead you out. For now is the time, my beautiful one.

The season has changed, the bondage of
your barren winter has ended, and the
season of hiding is over and gone.

—SONG OF SONGS 2:10–11 (TPT)

In October 1970, one month before I turned twenty-one, I gave my heart to Jesus. As I mentioned earlier, I was raised in a Christian home, and we went to church every time the doors were opened. However, I had never had a personal experience with Jesus. I always felt somehow that a holy God would not want me. I was so convicted by all my sins and misdeeds that I could never feel "good enough" to ask Him to come into my heart. You see, I had six siblings, and I was number six in the birth order. I always felt that my baby brother got my parents attention the most, and then my older brothers and sisters got what was left. I was always pushed aside and ignored. Now, I'm sure that's not the way it really was, but that's the way I saw it as I was growing up. Consequently, I became very rebellious as a teenager. I wanted nothing to do with God or with church. I couldn't wait to turn eighteen so I could move out of my parents' home, and that was exactly what I did. What I hadn't planned on was being a mother at eighteen. I put my parents through the embarrassment of my being pregnant and unmarried at seventeen. Because of their involvement and positions in our church, this was very hard on them.

James was the father of my child, but we were so young, and neither of us wanted to get married at that time. I left home and went to stay with my oldest sister and her family in Oregon. This was where my daughter, Perri Lynn, was born, two weeks before my eighteenth birthday. She was a beautiful baby, and I was so proud of her. I couldn't wait for James to see her and knew he would be proud of her too. I wasn't sure how that would happen because I had moved so far away.

My parents sold their home in California and joined me in Oregon just before Perri was born. My dad tried to find work there or even in Northern California so that we could live in a new place and I could have a fresh start, but he was not successful. My parents wanted to spare me the shame of having to face friends and church members back in California and explain my situation to them. However, God had another plan.

After a few months of my dad trying to find work with no success, we moved back to our hometown in California. God was directing my life every step of the way. Having my daughter was the best thing that ever happened to me. Now I had a little life depending on me, and I knew I needed to start making better life choices. This thought was at the center of everything I did, yet I was so guilt-ridden that I couldn't see any way to make my life right with a holy God.

What a lie and scheme of the devil to keep me from salvation! But on that Sunday morning in October, I had an encounter with Jesus that changed all that. A couple of years had passed since I had had my daughter. James and I were married now, and we had our first son, James, in that same year. Even though I didn't think God would accept me, I still went to church every Sunday. I didn't go thinking I could persuade God to accept me, but I went because I had two small children, and I wanted them to have a relationship with God. Perhaps they would not make the mistakes I had made. Also, now that James and I were married, I wanted to see him give his heart to Jesus. I knew that somehow, I had to be the example for my family.

On that particular Sunday morning, I was attending a little Baptist church in Norwalk, California, and we had a visiting evangelist preaching the message. I really can't remember any of his message, but at the end he gave an altar call for those who would like to receive Jesus into their hearts. I was standing at the back of the sanctuary and holding my firstborn son, who was three months old at that time. All of a sudden, I saw an open vision of Jesus in the altar. I couldn't see His face clearly because He was covered in something that looked like warm honey flowing over Him. But I knew that He was looking straight at me, and His arms were stretched out to me. I felt pure love and acceptance flowing from Him and coming toward me like ripples on a pond when you throw in a stone. I began to cry, and my whole body trembled. I looked to the young couple standing to my left and I asked them if they would hold my baby. As they took little James from me, I stepped out into the aisle and began to walk toward the vision.

As I moved forward, the vision disappeared, but I knew that Jesus was telling me by the love flowing to me that He had chosen me for His own. I was responding to that invitation of His love by going to the altar. His love was drawing me there. I had never felt such perfect, unconditional love in my life. I always felt like I had to perform to win the love and acceptance of others, but not with Jesus. It was amazing!

The next Sunday morning, I was baptized in that little church. Various people came up to me after the baptism and told me that I was literally glowing as I went into those baptismal waters. I was not at all surprised because I felt ecstatic following my Lord Jesus in baptism. I had never known this kind of love before, and I never wanted it to stop.

One would think that after such a wonderful experience, I wouldn't have wanted anything else to do with the temptations of this world, but that was not the case. My husband was raised Catholic and had served as an altar boy when he was young, but currently he was not attending church. He would allow me to take the children to the Baptist church, but he had no interest in going with us. I knew he would not understand if I tried to tell him about my experience, so I kept it to myself. I felt that if he knew I had this spiritual experience resulting in my giving my heart to Jesus, he would think me a religious fanatic and perhaps leave me. In an attempt to hold my marriage together, I began to live a double life. I know now that was a scheme of the devil to plant fear in my heart so I would not walk out my new life in Christ, and it worked for twelve years.

During that time, I continued to take the children to church on Sunday, but on Friday or Saturday night, I was usually with my husband in a bar or at a party. Our marriage had so many problems, and I had suspicions that he was being unfaithful, though the whole time God remained faithful to me. He answered my prayers and would at times overwhelm me with His loving presence. I found such comfort in His Word and loved to read it and share it with others.

Finally, I came to a point where I couldn't stand living that double life anymore, one foot in the world alongside my husband and the other foot in church. I wanted to be all in for Jesus, holding nothing back. The things of this world did not satisfy; they left me feeling empty and unfulfilled.

At that time, I rededicated my life to the Lord and told Him that I wanted to live only for Him from that day forward. A few weeks later, James followed suite and gave his heart to Jesus. Sometimes I think that if I had been totally committed to Jesus from the beginning, maybe James would have come to the Lord sooner.

As I reflect over the story of my life, I can see God's love demonstrated toward me in the ways that He has cared for and protected me all along the way, even when I was unaware of it. No one has ever loved me like Jesus does, and it humbles me when I think about it. He demonstrated His love for the whole world in what He did at Calvary, but each day, that divine demonstration of love can be seen by each one of us individually if we look for it. We don't have to look very hard.

> Dear friends, let us love one another, for love
> comes from God. Everyone who loves has
> been born of God and knows God. Whoever

does not love does not know God, because God is love. (1 John 4:7–8 NIV)

God indeed is love! His very essence is love. It's a tangible love that you can literally feel. If you ever come in contact with it, you will never forget it. You will be forever changed. Some are changed drastically, all at once, whereas others are changed gradually over a period of time. Whether drastically or gradually, all of us who encounter Him in this way are continually being changed because He is always at work in us, taking us from one degree of glory to another (2 Corinthians 3:18).

The love of our heavenly Father is so great for His children that He never considers the cost too great. Whatever it takes, He is willing to pay. The cost for our redemption was every drop of the precious blood of Jesus, and He willingly paid it. In my mind, I can't fathom that kind of love. If I hadn't experienced it for myself, I would never be able to believe that a holy God would care so deeply for me. I heard the message of His love Sunday after Sunday as a child, but I never thought it applied to me until I had that personal encounter with Him.

Now that I know and understand that God not only loves the whole world but also cares very deeply for each one of us personally, I have noticed little demonstrations of His love all around me.

For example, I truly enjoy beautiful sunsets. I could just sit and stare at them. I want to take in the grandeur of each one of them and not miss one detail. There have been times in my life that the sunsets were so beautiful, I was convinced that God painted them just for my eyes to behold. My relationship with Him is that personal. I would see a sunset as I was driving home from a stressful day at work, and it would lift my spirit and bring a smile to my face as I quietly said to Him, "Oh, Lord, You are showing off today, aren't You? You know how to bring a smile to my face. Thank You for this beautiful work of art."

I feel the need to pause and interject this: I know that God does not personally paint sunsets each day. The colors displayed in the sky have to do with air molecules, chemicals in the air, and a variety of other laws of physics. However, God is the one who created all those things and determined how they should interact with each other. I believe He did so in a way that would cause the eyes of all humanity to be drawn upward toward heaven each and every day and cause our hearts to seek after the Maker of heaven and earth. In other words, I think He chose to make sunsets beautiful in order to get our attention. The psalmist David expressed it this way: "The heavens proclaim the glory of God. The skies display His craftsmanship" (Psalm 19:1 NLT).

Another thing that God does for me concerns the turtle dove. From the time I first separated from James and moved into my own home until the present time, there has been a turtle dove every place that I have lived. At first there was a pair of doves, but one flew away; I believe this one represented my divorce. Then there was just one sitting on my fence. Whether I lived in California or Texas or stayed with my son in Montana, I would see a dove from time to time, either on my fence or sitting on my roof.

I've heard it said that turtle doves mate for life. My first conclusion concerning the birds was that God was giving me a symbol that James and I would be restored and would be together for life. However, when a single dove kept appearing even after James had passed away, I got quiet before the Lord and asked Him to please explain to me the constant appearance of the dove. I don't believe in coincidences, and this happened on such a regular basis that I knew there was a message for me in the appearance of the dove. I didn't want to miss it.

> For God may speak in one way, or in another,
> yet man does not perceive it. (Job 33:14 NKJV)

I am a visual learner; God created me that way. So many times, He speaks to me using visual aids. I knew this must be such a time. The following is what He spoke to my heart.

In the natural realm, the turtle dove symbolizes enduring love and faithfulness. That's why they are released during wedding ceremonies. In the Bible, it is sometimes used as a term of endearment for one that is deeply loved and cherished.

> O my dove, in the clefts of the rock, in the
> secret places of the cliff, let me see your face,

DOROTHY PINO

let me hear your voice; For your voice is sweet, and your face is lovely. (Song of Solomon 2:14 NKJV)

Therefore, the turtle dove that often appears outside my window is a symbol of Jesus to me. His love endures forever; He remains faithful even when I am not. His words to me are sweet, even if He's bringing correction, and His face or presence is indeed lovely.

He has chosen to send a turtle dove to remind me that He is with me, He is committed to me, and He will never leave me or forsake me. I am not alone. He calls me, via the Holy Spirit that is within me, into places of intimacy with Him. There are truths from His Word that He wants to reveal, answers to questions that I have had, and insights into things that are coming so I won't be caught unprepared. God does not desire to withhold information from us, but it requires a willingness on our part to come into that secret place with Him when He calls us there. So many times, we let the business of this life or our own agendas distract us, and we put Him off. We may not realize that is what we're doing until we sense His presence withdraw from us. Then there is an inner knowing that we have just missed a divine opportunity by not responding to His call to come away with Him. Oh, but He will call us to that place again another time. You can be sure of it. His love for us is steadfast, constantly reaching out to us and calling us deeper. What an amazing God!

8

I Will Not Fear

*For God has not given us a spirit of fear, but
of power and of love and of a sound mind.*
—2 Timothy 1:7 (NKJV)

When I left my husband and filed for divorce, I became very fearful. That is how the enemy was able to surround me with darkness. By listening to Satan's lies that I could not make it without James, and also that God had not been there for me, I stepped out of a place of faith and into fear. The devil had me right where he wanted me; I was totally deceived. He had brought in the fog so thick that I could no longer hear the leading of the Holy Spirit or even understand the scripture when I tried to read. When I prayed, it felt as though my prayers were going nowhere, but I am so thankful to God that my deliverance was not up to me; He never gives up on me.

> He giveth power to the faint; and to them that
> have no might He increases strength. (Isaiah
> 40:29 KJV)

When it seems as though everything around us is crumbling down and life isn't going the way we planned, all we have to do is hold on to His hand and refuse to let go. When we feel we are ready to faint, He will fight for us; when we are weak, He is strong on our behalf. He knows us better than we know ourselves, and He has promised to bring us through every adversity if we only believe. If we stay in a place of faith and refuse to fear no matter what, the devil can't have any victory against us.

As I am writing this book, the pandemic known as COVID-19 has invaded my nation and many nations around the world. The United States is on lockdown, with limited movement. Only those who work a job that is classified as "essential" are allowed to work, and many of them are working from home. The life that we knew just a few short weeks ago does not exist any longer. We are constantly hearing the phrase "This is the new norm." In other words, even when the virus is wiped out, there are some things that will never go back to the way they were before this pandemic invaded our world.

When things shift so quickly in a negative way, people feel insecure and become fearful. If our world can change so drastically overnight, then where do we anchor our hope? Because it is human nature to put our hope in things that give us a sense of security, some have put their hope in their jobs or paychecks, in their investments or retirement accounts, or in their homes and family support to always be there for them. All these things can fail us. These things are of the material realm and are always changing. The only thing in this world that remains constant is Jesus. He is the same yesterday, today, and forever (Hebrews 13:8). Because He never changes, we can count on Him to be there for us no matter what we face. That is a promise in His Word (Hebrews 13:5).

God did not bring this deadly virus into the earth; this is the work of Satan. But God can turn it for good in our lives if we only believe and do not fear. In John 10: 10 (NIV), Jesus says, "The thief comes only to steal and kill and destroy; I have come that they may have life and have it to the full."

The only real weapon Satan has against humankind is deception. Through deception, he brings in fear. Perhaps you are familiar with the following acrostic.

False
Evidence
Appearing
Real

I'm not sure where it originated, but it paints a very clear picture of fear.

Fear is crippling. Once we give place to it, we are no longer being led by God but by the devil and the spirit of fear that comes from him. Jesus tells us, "I leave the gift of peace with you, my peace. Not the kind of fragile peace given by the world, but my perfect peace. Don't yield to fear or be troubled in your hearts—instead, be courageous" (John 14:27 TPT)

We are also told, "Love never brings fear, for fear is always related to punishment. But love's perfection drives the fear of punishment far from our hearts" (1 John 4:18a TPT).

I am so thankful that fear has no place in the heart of a true, born-again believer. Fear is never from God! When the enemy comes against us with his plots and our hearts are tempted to be afraid, we need only remember that God is on our side, and Satan has already been defeated (Colossians 2:15). Jesus defeated him at Calvary, and all we have to do is enforce the victory that has already been won. We do this by the words of our mouths, speaking the promises of God from the Bible and not the negative words of the situation going on around us. We choose whose words we are going to believe.

As we stand in faith on the promises of God, peace is the natural outcome, and it is a peace that passes all understanding. People may ask us how we can have peace in the midst of the turmoil and uncertainty in the world, and we can tell them about our Jesus and invite them to know Him too.

A Prayer for Salvation

For God so loved the world that He gave His
only begotten Son, that whoever believes in
Him should not perish but have everlasting
life. For God did not send His Son into the
world to condemn the world, but that the
world through Him might be saved.

—John 3:16–17 (NKJV)

He died for our sins and rose again to make us
right with God, filling us with God's goodness.

—Romance 4:25 (TLB)

For whoever calls on the name of the Lord
shall be saved.

—Romans 10:13 (NKJV)

If you would like to receive Jesus as your Savior, pray this
simple prayer from your heart: "Dear Lord Jesus, I believe
that You died for me. I ask You to come into my heart and
be my Savior. Fill me with Your Holy Spirit and give me the
power to live my life for You. Amen."

CPSIA information can be obtained
at www.ICGtesting.com
Printed in the USA
LVHW111554040221
678382LV00019B/684

9 781664 211780